A Tree and Gone

℘

TERENCE CULLETON

FUTURECYCLE PRESS
www.futurecycle.org

Cover artwork, "Brother's Tree," by Nita C. Lescher; author photo by Nancy Culleton; cover and interior book design by Diane Kistner; Georgia text with Acherus Grotesque titling

Library of Congress Control Number: 2021932527

Published by FutureCycle Press
Athens, Georgia, USA

ISBN 978-1-952593-13-0

For Nancy

tree not gone, always in flower

A Color stands abroad
On Solitary Fields
That Science cannot overtake
But Human Nature feels.

It waits upon the Lawn,
It shows the furthest Tree
Upon the furthest Slope you know
It almost speaks to you.

—Emily Dickinson,
  "A Light exists in Spring" (812)

Contents

1.
Acadia

2.
A Tree and Gone

3.

After the Melt

1.
Acadia

Fudge Shop

Whorling in a pot of scrumptious muck,
the ladle thwupped and diligently clacked
against the copper, or it scraped and struck
bottom as desire against some fact
will claw to speak of sweetness in the world.
The aproned cook, primly stolid, leaned
into her task as the confection swirled
into itself and nothing intervened
between itself and its deliciousness
inbreeding in that solipsistic pot.
The more of it kept cooking down to less,
and even less, until a thickened lot
sat rounded at the bottom of the kettle,
convex in a concavity of metal.

Beach Ball

Shanked sparkling off a toe out to the tide,
it bobbed along from crest to crest ashore,
and we ran out to meet it, satisfied
with getting back what we'd possessed before:
a brilliance we returned at once to play,
caressing, bopping it—and, nudged or flung,
it bounced heroically along the spray
as if it meant to reign supreme among
umbrellas, castles, coolers, sandy knees.
It might have been pride punched it then aloft,
for it was lifted on a landward breeze
transversely down the dunes beyond the soft
sea grass, then dropped plumb into salt-marsh slime
from which it would not be returned this time.

In Sequent Toil

The little story of a wave concludes
in clumps of foam about a toddler's knees
to tell the denouement of landward moods
in one last moiling. Cold redundancies,
more waves spend their force—to draw back and
erase themselves: it's safe for her to kneel
and slap at them and scoop up gobs of sand
to fondle or find gritty, at the feel
of which she makes a sourpuss face and cries
as at the wind or sun-glints off the sea,
then looks back up the beach to fix her eyes
on pale-faced parents leaning hungrily
into *The Times* to keep track of a war
they don't approve of and will not ignore.

Penultimate

Down at the blind end of the breezeway Lust
incarnate in a vase of peonies
perpetrates a Cha Cha on a gust,
singing love has brought it to its knees.
Like you it wants to marry everything
and never ever would divorce its kind.
It larkifies it's tethered on a string
of gold lamé to your heart, you're entwined
with it—warbles and throbs that your affection
is a sanctifying dream of ocean light,
as now the sea breeze loses its direction
as it did a time or two throughout the night
and Lust stands still—so I'm inclined to go
upstairs, and wake you up, and let you know.

Fisherman

The spangled red-gold vasty deep wet dream
spread out before him lures his sky-prone pole
down toward it, so it arcs, as it would seem,
over the spring tide shoving in to roll
and gush and shudder on the foam-glossed sand
and then pull surely back with a feral hiss
as if taking the spunk out of the land
forever and for its own purposes.
Even his line sags in the afterglow
of sunset. Buckets of chunked bait deployed
behind him make an unconvincing show
of more work to be done. A gull hangs buoyed
above the breakers, then sheers off to cry
anticlimactically against the sky.

Beach Development

The eye looks past fences and lawn toys for less:
myrtles nestled there among the dunes,
unimpeded swaths of ocean cress,
seagrass wagging where the wind maroons
itself and whispers to itself and sighs,
and everything becoming what it is
for good, unmindful, though appraising eyes
might place a speculative emphasis
on what the mind *could* take all this to be.
The ocean spreads itself across the sand.
Up here the sand rises: you can see
the way it comes alive in storm light and
tosses itself on gusts, as love might toss
itself away—for profit or for loss.

Dune Cottage

It hunches slantwise in the gale-force wind;
the crazy kitchen door flies open, shuts
again, slamming on some message dinned
into the buckled shingles as to what's
ahead for it—ahead for anything
at the verge like that, teetering on its sill.
Time's claim is tidal, so its settling
is nothing but a braving on until
the whelming sure to come. It isn't song
just to stand the brunt of such a fury
keeping shuttered council all along,
and neither, strictly speaking, is it story,
because it knows no plot. It will not rhyme
but only hold together for a time.

Auguries

Beach break moils and shrugs up just the same
as back when (I remember) all were here
deployed and laughing at some paddle game.
Terns flock the padlocked fishing pier
like souls, oblivious to boundaries.
The wind keens round as if to crack my face
from my skull. Gulls mill about with knotted knees
high in the upwash. Some complain, some race
up here and past, suddenly caring for
a thing I'd never know or—as I'd guess—
think of, some crab leg like a metaphor
that can't say what it is. My life's a mess.
It was never meant to be, but is, and here
is where I've come with it and what I fear.

Last Dip

Feeling all this next week away from it
won't be the same, but it will have to be
(standing in line for scrips or asked to sit
with a magazine unflexed across a knee)—
to feel this at that moment, this un-urgent
swell and heave and throb as now you ride
it in all over, whelmed by the resurgent
piling on and crashing of the tide.
It won't be real enough. But isn't this
already only *just* enough? The mind,
washed up, clears, thinks it hears the suck and hiss
almost of blood where waves draw back behind
themselves a wrack of sea scum green and brown,
and there is nothing but a thought to drown.

No Sea of Faith

A light like cold glass flats splintering
as daylight drops around a pail of bait
and the scene resigns itself to wintering
landward January cloud banks great
with the predicted snow squall coming on.
Gulls wild it, rising balkily, to fall
also balkily, and hunger-drawn
to where there isn't any food at all.
Waves shrug, pulling back, draw up, and lunge,
and seethe, and haul themselves back out again,
hunching and shrugging some more before they plunge
back in and seethe, withdraw, and always then
the same old out and beetling back to shore
imbecilic—as each time before.

Acadia

High-keeled small-catch boats out in the harbor
breast the current, if there's one to breast,
while here kids stretch gum strands across an arbor
and their parents take a moment off to rest
from too much shopping, maybe, too much sun.
This afternoon they'll hit the gentler trails,
the ones that loop around so when you're done
you're "back" and only weariness prevails,
not any sense of loss. —Who gave it all
away, one wonders, pushing up the hard
unyielding climbs, at some brave heart-chord call
of an eagle, or a falcon flying guard:
Who gave it all away? And how—and why?
Who put it here to visit in July?

Photographing Hoodoos (Bryce Canyon)

Thou still unravished bride...
—John Keats

As of yet these, too, are still unravished or
too slowly carved to call it ravishing.
Distended, urn-like, rust-red, eighteen soar
above me as I inch down, ogling.
Some seem countenanced like totem poles
or tiki men atilt to ruminate
as I square round to frame their limestone souls
within the finder lest the inner state
of stone be only stone, what wind and hail
have carved respond as nothing to the eye.
And I'll insist on thinking up the tale
of what I see here—now—and maybe why
I found them this way, beautiful, and true
as anything I've known or thought I knew.

Out on Ascension Point

Skies dissolve only to reappear
in time, blinding ascendancies of light,
no clouds at all, just empty atmosphere,
a hawk or two stretched out in tipsy flight
above the desert. Then an endlessness
of stars revolves above diluvial
driftings—shingle, rodent carcasses
dried flat in time's insistent protocol.
Light again, and heat, another day
and no strict difference if these toys of death
are here or not—anything we say
is really just a luxury of breath:
we gaze straight up into the photon bath
above us all and all this aftermath.

Selskar Abbey (County Wexford)

Can't but admit I found this place to feel
peace in all its rubble, rock by rock,
clambering: here, if you stop and kneel
on one knee at around, say, two o'clock,
you'll see the brown rune-chiseled cross gone gold
with flaring in the sun; you'll feel it all,
the rites that echoed, all the bells, the old
grand transubstantiating folderol
at rest. At last. The peace, at last, of death.
Something, though, disturbs me, even here,
where prayer seems preternatural as breath
and ruin's coldly piled up atmosphere
is charged with its own past, which, after all,
sleeps fitfully upon its own downfall.

Peekaboo Falls

They weren't on the guidebook's "Must See" list:
I trekked as to a mystery to be solved
and stood below the cold cascading mist
into which the sluicing rush devolved
halfway down. Falls in magazines
compound themselves in thunderous aftershocks
but these un-photogenic smithereens
hovered in air above the glossy rocks,
unfazed by what they'd been, self-overthrown,
playing hide-and-seek—their turn to hide—
then reassembling on the scooped limestone
to chuckle straight down the mountainside,
wavelets glinting my way knowingly
as if they'd shared some sort of joke with me.

River Reeds

A month or so ago, strong wind or storm
surged over them and bent them as in prayer.
In aftermath they hold that moment's form.
Shagged with clumps of something like mohair,
they sparkle and the ice groans with the flow
under a low sky smudging into black
and all the air smells like a night of snow,
which makes me think I'd better get on back.
Come spring, another surge will break the spell
to bully them out of this symmetry,
but what tonight I'll think about as well
is how they seem to strain obsessively
to find that out that found them out and feel
in straining that what bent them is still real.

More So This River

No man ever steps in the same river twice...
—Heraclitus

Each day, it seems to me, it's just like this.
Down reach, out past the highway overpass
(trucks hump across, hydraulic systems hiss),
it's dark but sparkles, too, like leaded glass.
Along the other bank, black willows sway
among strict stands of purple river cane
as waves pulse in around them murky grey.
All twinkles and refracts out in the main
where a little island is, a little hut
where someone used to live, I guess, but now
it's all graffitied up and tinged with soot.
Someone might live there sometimes anyhow.
If so, how strange to come out, cold and small,
and stand midstream amazed about it all.

2.
A Tree and Gone

The Woods of Saxony

Outlandish notion for a housing tract,
the ring of it surreal, or just not real,
really—counterfactual, in fact.
Fiction, I guess, holds true as curb appeal.
I don't drive through. I'd leave the area
untested by mundane experience,
leave its strange untenable idea
of itself intact—its crazy self-known sense:
Saxons trudge along a quiet street
in bearskins, war hammers in their hands.
Housewives shriek and fly in shocked retreat
as husbands run to make heroic stands:
rakes clash on helms, sit-mowers flame and roar
like dragons—fateful still—in Eddic lore.

Viparinama

A droop-eyed, round-jowled, ringleted Buddha's head
presides upon a riser, on display
here in the window, unaware a red-
sweatered fashion dummy by a hay
bale in the clothes shop straight across Oak Street
stares blankly at him through the plate
glass glare. Buddha has no arms, trunk, feet,
the dummy has no soul. Both seem sedate.
It's fall, and shopping season once again.
This little New Age book store has its stream
of votaries, who browse and nod, and then
cross to chase that other window-dream.
The weeks will come on colder soon, and wetter.
Souls will each require a brilliant sweater.

Outside the Mall

I've heard once all of this was pasture land,
paved over now, marked out in lanes and grids
so cars may graze. What I don't understand
is why some planner double-clicked orchids
for planting here, as it turns out, beneath
a banner sign showing three girls in bras
laughing cannily with gleaming teeth.
What sun we get would best suit zinnias,
as would the base precipitation rate,
but orchids bob and weave as if they knew
that not succeeding is a kind of fate
money brings anything worth anything to:
herds, flocks, wildflowers startled on a knoll
once, here, somewhere—the heart, maybe, the soul.

Empirical

—for C. L. Dodgson

If what I only know is all I know,
why want to know the things I know at all?
Strange thought to think just here, but on I go
vaguely around a rundown shopping mall,
wanting to angle myself back outside
across the parking lot past cars in rows
to one small patch that they'll have failed to hide
with tar, and maybe find a tumtum grows,
which, well, impossible. Don't need the books,
the downloads, links, fact-based things I see
on "readers" e-rudite in coffee nooks
to know, Dodgson, there's really no such tree.
Whatever. I'm gone through the airlock door
to find what I'd find out there—maybe more.

Across and Back

I saw sunlight suffuse huge shags of grass
there on the median and half believed
that in the purview of an overpass
a metaphor for love might be perceived,
though I was not inclined to let it be
quite that and felt the urge to reconstrue
my passion as a kind of fantasy
in seeing romance on Route Sixty-Two
along the cloverleaf. But stalks like necks
stretched up beneath the dusk (later the night)
across from yet another multiplex,
and I decided my first thought was right
or ought to be—pure as it was, and sweet
to contemplate, and wholly incomplete.

Quasi-Darwinian

A peacock butterfly unfolds on air
and glides a yard or two, then re-alights
atop a primrose bell to bristle there
and fold back in and think about its flights,
I'd guess—how bright they've seemed, and passing strange
in light of erstwhile caterpillarings,
if it could conjure them. Now, at close range,
a robin chirps just as this wonder flings
itself off somewhere else and doesn't know
it's being watched by eyes that stop to see,
in the flash of its eyed wings, a patterned woe
to predatory beaks—also to me,
taught to read into such patterning
protection from a scarlet-breasted thing.

Heaven

I'd say it was a second's second guess
that made me gaze up at the lovely sky
today and think about its loveliness.
A kind of absent-minded wondering why
the all of it was in its essence blue
became the question. This was what I thought
some years ago I'd learned and therefore knew
based on the simple science I'd been taught:
the ether's molecules conspired to let
only the light's blue wavelengths penetrate,
so they were what I saw. I knew that, yet
it seemed less easy to affirm than state,
like feeling chemicals instead of love
or not conceiving of some world above.

A Tree and Gone

A sudden prepossessing pinkish tree
haunted the roadside as I shuttled north,
tending west of where I had to be
at the end of all my driving back and forth.
Could I have dreamt it there above that swale,
its petals puffed out roseate in the sun?
The haze of all of it seemed like a veil
not to be lifted up by anyone.
I'm sure I wasn't sleeping at the wheel,
but then again I could have been. The tree
seemed old and, for suburbia, surreal.
Then it was past, and, kind of glad to be
past it, I focused on the road and all
the vinyl clarity of tract and sprawl.

Unleaving

Its whole load dumped, the big tree stands at last
having itself to love for what it has
or not: a self without the self it cast
down like so much gaudy razzmatazz
of leafage lost. What's left in stark relief
against the blue is just a circuitry.
Its summer charge was radiant and brief.
I, for one, believed in it. For me
the thought held true that it would never pass
and that the tree would be allowed to hold
to what I thought its un-thought compound mass.
Folly, of course. And so I'm getting old.
What self-possession's left is to be glad
it's what it is—had what it ever had.

One Apple

—after Thoreau and Bishop

This shock of yellow crab-fall, where the lawn
denies the path due access, states a case
for summer's grinding down again to gone
as the season of its grinding takes its place—
"season" for the fact that it provides
a fruit that is its own to give, its own
sweet-sour or smoky odors. Pesticides
or not, the click of split skin, that alone,
not even counting in the scrabbled chill
mash of all of it cramming down a throat
that wants to choke against it, trains the will
to one simple art: as if by rote
to know that all's soon gone, nor think it sad
that what one has stands in for what one had.

Spruce

A sapling fenced about with chicken wire
stood in a field of milkweed everywhere,
and meadow grass and woodbine, gypsy briar
and wild bamboo. Someone had taken care
to come from town to stake, as round a grave,
a stinted fence shaped like a battered horn
around the trunk, so that the tree seemed brave
in its confinement, as a unicorn
heroically lamenting bygone magic
might stand contained and drop a silver tear.
But nothing in suburbia is tragic:
the fence fenced out the famished nibbling deer
to give the young tree freedom to apprise
itself of wind and light and bottle flies.

Subdivision Willow

Its wind-crazed self-containment stakes a claim
upon a patch of land not gobbled whole
by money, which will eat it all the same
next year, perhaps, and so play out its role
in speeding up time's gentler battening.
Not wands, but braided, cataracting coils
backlit in shadow, tresses on a fling,
ride upgusts or snap to among great spoils
of oak leaves whorling skyward off the street:
a tree encompassed by its shagginess,
disheveled as the sky and indiscreet
as some old virgin lifting up her dress,
or anything whose nature knows no bound
in gloating over uncontracted ground.

Hermetic

I'd like to go by climbing a birch tree...
—Robert Frost

The sense of it is only understood
if I consider it outside of time:
a scored trunk soaring, me there wondering could
I climb higher than others might yet climb
(who didn't even want their names up there)
—then branches scratching, twigs and branches scraping,
the uppermost alive with light and air,
penknife digging into bark, shaping
letters other kids would never see,
clinging to unknowable renown
at last and, riding high there, only me
at the top of what months later would come down
when dozers cleared that tract of land I need
to think of still as theater to the deed.

Graveside

If ever there were sign that all that mud
would open up someday to what could come,
it might have been just one cloud like a bud
moiling and unfurling west, as some
might say the soul finds out its way to God.
And God saw all from up-where in the sky:
the wreaths and mounded chunks of sod,
us assembled there to say goodbye
with tossing Canna lilies on the lid.
God kept the very silence we all bore
because we had to, and the things we did
were but by way of saying something more
might come of it, some May-time afterglow,
which may come after all for all we know.

Meadow Stalks

They point away from where I'm jogging to
as I lean head down straight into the gale
as if against it. Just exactly who
I think I am they seem to know, these frail
cat stalks and blades, cotton-pods, shreds
and tufts of which, kachooed across the path,
bank along exhausted flower beds.
Pushing on in all this aftermath
of hot green days that even now survive
as memories of grass and sun and song
and everything unthinkingly alive,
this is my one way left of being strong,
and I will argue it against the wind
in stride, and striving, and undisciplined.

Six Miler

He keeps pace with his early times as though
he had it in him to outrun his age,
stomping down the towpath, crunching snow.
He must have some last fantasy to wage
against such mists as muster in the sky,
less like an army than a cataract
spread white across the universe's eye,
which is already blind to him, in fact.
He runs as if the place to which he ran
were all (the pain within parentheses).
He'll end up back at home where he began,
to edge around all night on gimpy knees,
complaining to the walls of hip and heel
but not defeat (the harder thing to feel).

Yin

One sector of the field gets everything
—great trapezoids of light and steady heat—
and there, eugenically, stand towering
proud battalions of deserving wheat
obedient to wind and undeterred
by frost or storm or late September drought,
or, lifting on an updraft, one bright bird
above a felt-knobbed buck puzzling about.
The yin's the shaded sector over there
of twisted stalks and weeds, a rock or two,
and other things impervious to glare—
ground mold, fungus, garter snakes, a blue-
tongued rat conniving by a clump of hay
to carry something decomposed away.

La Vie En Rose

You might like crackers smudged with fudge pâté,
sitting at a wrought-iron tabletop
in a shop you've come to like called *Chocolatté,*
waiting for the snow outside to stop.
You may like pralines or primroses or
the blush of pink against the darkened day,
the Paris-themed mosaic of the floor,
one last flaked confection on a tray.
You might think you've no right to like these things,
might think them faked-up luxuries, and think
—as somewhere lovelorn Edith Piaf sings—
one must not sit here happy in this pink
and precious hatbox, safe from the world out there
so cold and white and windy, and unfair.

Pre-Prandial

For lunch we sit uncertain at a table
set up with cutlery, crystal, fresh bread:
wobbly, though—the footing is unstable.
The more we say, the more we leave unsaid.
Nearby a fork keeps tapping at a plate.
Chords waft somewhere hazy as a cloud.
You take a roll—me, too. We hesitate.
A child nearby recites her name out loud.
Her voice is like a bird's that knows its name.
It's been six weeks since you tried suicide.
We chat a bit about the playoff game,
then silence, smiles. Violins collide
up in the cloud while quiet muffled drums
pulsate and, finally, here the waitress comes.

Misericordia Hospital Bus

The bundle hoisted to this mother's chin
is just a bundle, nothing more—nor less.
The cry against the grinding bus is thin,
one feels, and has its thinness to express,
the way a small fire bristling in the night
might not even warm itself or cast
so much as a sufficiency of light
to give one any faith that it will last.
Bangled arms engulf it under eyes
that seem to breathe in watching it, or dart
out the window for a quick surmise
as to the stop. The engine, like a heart
at prayer, pulses in the heartless red
of traffic ticking toward the merge ahead.

3.
After the Melt

Now Goldenrod

Compounds in piles and plumes of goldenrod,
so we've put off our paperwork to sit
lifting snifters to the minor god
inside a fondue pot of chocolate
here by a trellis mobbed and blossom-gilt.
Autumn's delayed this week: flags and chimes
and bugs and birds play happy to the hilt.
I'm game, too, for a few more happy times.
With you I hold my gold-rimmed glass straight up
to unpursed lips. It tips and tilts itself
the way unto a bee a buttercup
might tilt. —A bee, perhaps a mothwing elf,
or something of that unselfconscious class
for whom a season is a life to pass.

More, And Still More

—to John Keats

This leaf-blaze seems a kind of inquisition—
the heresy involved June's disbelief
in anything but song without contrition:
all things in time accommodate to grief.
You'd call the brilliance tragic, yes, but wise,
that autumn finds at last a faith as fair
as any trill or chutter—up it flies
like tongues of fire ascending as in prayer.
You'd mean, of course, the leaves. They swoop and soar
above me here. I listen, as I gaze,
as to a truth too steady to ignore
and also much too beautiful these days
to take for other than the songs of spring
giving way soon—but soon—to everything.

Stopped

I didn't want to think I saw it—just
breakage: scrappy leaves out in the wrack,
sticks whirling, only time at all to trust
to bring it all in time brilliantly back
come spring. I had to get somewhere by ten
and sat in traffic waiting for the light
to toggle green so I could go again.
My blinker said I would be merging right
as if that were the only thing to say
to all those cars behind me and beside.
This was a day like any other day.
I had to get there—get there—so to ride
unseeing through what-all there was to see
was, as I wished, just how it had to be.

Broken Red Ceramic Heart

Before the move I told myself to wrap
it carefully, box it, place it high
on a top-floor closet shelf, a packing strap
around it once or twice, to double-tie
the ends in furious knots—all which I did,
having also swaddled it in a shag
blanket, tied that with triple-ply braided
boat rope and put that in a vinyl bag
folded over twice and duct-taped. Now
four shards reflect the TV screen's blue light
kind of prettily. I don't know how
the damned thing fell, but, so, okay, it might
be fixed with glue, packed in excelsior,
and put back in the closet—on the floor.

Students Skating at Rockefeller Center

Some sheer around, some teeter on their skates
and push off to recover, others glide
half-hunkering through shaky figure eights.
Three hug the boards along the other side,
and one on this side readjusts his hat
to get a tighter fit. There's music, too,
some tape-looped bop tune cluttered up with scat.
Waiting here means nothing else to do
but watch them taxi hopefully. They seem
—if not Olympics bound—still, set to veer
toward *some* kind of glory, mouthing steam.
I'd like to be like them again, career
about in yellow gloves, red scarf, and all
those layers on for luck were I to fall.

One Way

The gist of everything was that they hid,
the skates, atop an upturned rocking chair
in a broken cardboard box without a lid
nestled on some throw rugs frayed with wear.
So if I wanted to go skate that day,
I had to clamber up the chockablock
pile of the family's past—now thrown away
to molder in its state of aftershock—
and pilfer them. The creek, a solid sheet
on which to fly off sucking air for good,
would whisper to my awkward-rhythmed feet
as I scraped up it through the ice-bright wood
straight toward a gelid reach, winter-blind
to what was up there—and what was behind.

Withheld

Each burr ball pendant from a knuckled twig
darkens inside itself as I walk by,
then turns bruise-black. They're meatball-sized, not big
against the moodiness that sweeps the sky,
and filled with seeds predestined for a spring
that will shine more accommodatingly.
The wind affects an endless bustling—
a fitful nurse—while Doctor Gravity,
as with forceps, grabs each slight bitter brain.
Tonight, tomorrow maybe, they will drop
and down will rain the cold November rain
without remorse or any thought to stop.
But as for now, as if some etiquette
required them to, they hang there brooding yet.

Winter Berries

I wonder if the deer still cluster round
at night to nose and munch among these twigs.
The only signs I see here on the ground
—hoared calculi dispersed among dry sprigs
of blackened pine, a rimed hoofprint or three—
suggest they've found another cache long since
and left these nodes bunched calmly in the lee
of winter's rhetoric, which *will* convince
me, at least, cold nourishment like this
is what there is at last. Here they can catch
the cloud light, which seems such an ambient bliss
to gleam and dangle in, each hardened batch
unheeded but by me, and I've come here
to reassure myself about the deer.

That Time of Year

Bare ruin'd choirs where late the sweet birds sang...
—Shakespeare, Sonnet 73

Angled and clean as cold communion arms,
these branches lift what's left to know of light
in ruthless glints, the choir being gone, its charms
unwarbled here beneath the moth-wing white
of winter, which unloves itself as well
and therefore cries and moans among the trees
as if it only had death-news to tell.
It carps and calls in balky, broken keys,
flinging its loneliness against the sky
to dissipate up there. —And I agree
with its offense and its relentless cry.
The counterpoint that sounds itself in me
just now, I guess, is yes, it's almost night—
but almost isn't all: there's still some light.

Gazebo

I'd go there with a sandwich in a bag,
a gnarled cheroot, a lidded cup of Joe.
I'd bring the dog, I'd watch her pitch and zag
in wafts and skirls of blindingly bright snow,
her beastly glad breaths pompadouring there
above her snout. And I would sit and watch
not only her but crows she'd rouse and scare
with her galumphings. —Or the butterscotch
of resin on a sheltered stump, or spears
of ice down-jabbing from the lattice work
along the eaves like little chandeliers.
The snow would twinkle, silently berserk,
then settle on the rail in one soft layer,
and I would have in mind a kind of prayer.

After the Melt

What's lost is how the starshine tinged it blue
once it had installed itself, almost
blotting out the world of straight and true,
obfuscating tree and rail and post.
It came as a bombardment on the town,
silently, faux Quaker style. Its light
consensus and the reason it came down
was in its falling wiftily and white.
But having dispossessed itself of speed
by way of frank possession of the streets,
and midnight being clear, and every weed
smothered, lawns tucked underneath its sheets,
it seemed to find in its possession true
peace in being just so slightly blue.

Ides

Everything or nothing comes around
today upon a sudden hungry wind
keening in the chimney. Such a sound
souls make, maybe, knowing that they've sinned,
as I believe against the spring I've done
by keeping everything inside myself.
The bay leaf jar taps at the cinnamon.
Stacks of cups and saucers on the shelf,
bowls as well, record the rattling
of screen door, rocker, porch, pane, and shutter.
The whole house seems fierce for battling
what peace I've waged against the urge to utter
with the March wind that tears its hair to sing
that I'd be through for now with wintering.

Amor Vincit Omnia

The wind is much too high not to remind
the shutters of their winter's worth of speech,
which they revive today as if to find
the one conclusion they all failed to reach
in their crude chatter-clash against the siding
throughout the tedious months. Who'd listen now
as logic yields to birdsong? Such confiding
relies on atmospherics anyhow—
against the sudden flowers red and blue,
it seems a cavil. Winter's nihilism,
compelling to the eye, turns hardly true
when May converts the eye to solipsism,
that kind cradle-rock of prayer and song
that can't be, in its own light, ever wrong.

Marsh Marigolds

They call it up, these star-clawed marigolds
in hordes come startlingly generous
to shock the eye with what the season holds
in store for you stopped and ogling thus.
Briefcase in hand along the thoroughfare,
you sport perhaps a fat or florid tie
or jaunty hat, or even underwear
printed with hearts. And these, to verify
the world is still as fresh as it once was,
wag themselves and trip out on the breeze
as if for some grand and utopian cause.
They're yellow, urgent, loud as what from trees
disheveled by a sudden after-gust
trills down all throatiness and tufted lust.

A Fancy

What I heard up high came down as stuttered clucks
and screaks bespeaking sudden happiness.
I thought a set of hens or hen-like ducks
had something epiphanic to express
up there among the twigs, their earthbound souls
unquiet in that stratosphere of light.
But then I saw—what?—six grey orioles
flustering up and darting off in flight,
finding an apex, then in scattershot
disappearing past a farther tree
as I walked on across the parking lot,
wondering why it had occurred to me
that such an odd displacement could occur:
that ducks could lose their sense of what they were.

The Confidence

Flecked trumpet bells, ground boscage lightly jeweled
and cobweb-laced upon the wet dark moss—
my sound sleep had been soundly overruled
by trills, and I'd roused out to cut my loss
while no one else was up. The sky filled all
its capillaries with a fleeting blush.
Honeysuckle surged across the wall,
and I'll be damned if that wasn't a thrush
hunched in among green twinings and now mute
at my approach, but throbbing anyway
and eyeing me in front of it. A shoot
of chickweed caught a dropping, which was grey
as gone-stale grout, and then the bird beaked brief
chansons, enunciating a belief.

Blessing

—after James Wright

A red roan Appaloosa moseys to the rail
and pokes her nose across at me to snuff
some sweet hay in my fist, switching her tail
as her eyes cross to focus on the stuff
the better in the dim air. Stars are out,
a few at least, and, too, the orange moon
has cleared the trees. It shines here on her snout
as she draws up her lip. The ground is strewn
with clumps of hay placed for the eating. She
prefers instead to nuzzle at my hand
as if these tufts pertained to mystery,
as she to me pertains, stunned where I stand
unclenching all, here, now, only to live
for giving her what isn't mine to give.

Acknowledgments

These poems have appeared in the following magazines and journals:

Antiphon: "Graveside"
Better Than Starbucks: "Viparanama" [Featured Poem]
Blue Unicorn: "Unleaving"
The Eclectic Muse: "Marigolds," "A Tree and Gone," "Across and Back"
Innisfree: "Six Miler"
The Lyric: "Penultimate," "Ides"
Making Our Own Light: "More, And Still More"
Orbis: "Blessing," "Fudge Shop"
Raintown Review: "One Apple"
Rat's Ass Review: "Spruce"
The Road Not Taken: "Dune Cottage," "Beach Development," "The Fisherman"
Schuylkill Valley Journal: "Gazebo," "Outside the Mall," "Anti-Darwinian," "Beachball," "Yin"
Sparks of Calliope: "Amor Vincit Omnia," "Meadow Stalks"

"Fudge Shop" received 1st Honorable Mention in the 2019 Helen Schaible International Traditional Sonnet Contest.

About FutureCycle Press

FutureCycle Press is dedicated to publishing lasting English-language poetry in both print-on-demand and Kindle (eBook) formats. Founded in 2007 by long-time independent editor/publishers and partners Diane Kistner and Robert S. King, the press incorporated as a nonprofit in 2012. A number of our editors are distinguished poets and writers in their own right, and we have been actively involved in the small press movement going back to the early seventies.

We award the FutureCycle Poetry Book Prize and honorarium annually for the best full-length volume of poetry we published that year. Introduced in 2013, proceeds from our Good Works projects are donated to charity. Our Selected Poems series highlights contemporary poets with a substantial body of work to their credit; with this series we strive to resurrect work that has had limited distribution and is now out of print.

We are dedicated to giving all of the authors we publish the care their work deserves, offering a catalog of the most diverse and distinguished work possible, and paying forward any earnings to fund more great books. All of our books are kept "alive" and available unless and until an author requests a title be taken out of print.

We've learned a few things about independent publishing over the years. We've also evolved a unique and resilient publishing model that allows us to focus mainly on vetting and preserving for posterity poetry collections of exceptional quality without becoming overwhelmed with bookkeeping and mailing, fundraising activities, or taxing editorial and production "bubbles." To find out more about what we are doing, come see us at www.futurecycle.org.

The FutureCycle Poetry Book Prize

All full-length volumes of poetry published by FutureCycle Press in a given calendar year are considered for the annual FutureCycle Poetry Book Prize. This allows us to consider each submission on its own merits, outside of the context of a traditional contest. Too, the judges see the finished book, which will have benefitted from the beautiful book design and strong editorial gloss we are famous for.

The book ranked the best in judging is announced as the prize-winner in the subsequent year. There is no fixed monetary award; instead, the winning poet receives an honorarium of 20% of the total net royalties from all poetry books and chapbooks the press sold online in the year the winning book was published. The winner is also accorded the honor of being on the panel of judges for the next year's competition; all judges receive copies of all contending books to keep for their personal library.

www.ingramcontent.com/pod-product-compliance
Lightning Source LLC
Chambersburg PA
CBHW070010100426
42741CB00012B/3183